Poems, Prose and Prayers

A Lifetime of Reflection

Julia Frazier White, Ph.D.
Illustrated by Cheryl Ann White

Library of Congress Control Number:		2014901759
ISBN:	Hardcover	978-1-4931-6810-1
	Softcover	978-1-4931-6811-8
	eBook	978-1-4931-6809-5

Print information available on the last page.

Rev. date: 01/28/2016

To order additional copies of this book, contact:
Xlibris
1-888-795-4274
www.Xlibris.com
Orders@Xlibris.com
549381

Dedication

This book is gratefully dedicated to loved ones.

To my dear departed father, Latham Norvell Frazier, for his gentle nature, constant encouragement, and unconditional love. I eagerly read my poems to him because he always voiced his appreciation, saying, "You are so creative." It made me feel so important.

To my precious departed mother, Alyce Brewer Frazier for always loving me and teaching me so many things about life. Mother taught us the love for poetry, prose, and prayers. She taught us to memorize the works of her favorite authors. The very first memory piece Mother taught us was Psalm 23 and it is included in this book. At an early age, we memorized very long poems with good lessons for living.

Mother and Daddy listened to our prayers at night.

My children have encouraged me to write. They have inspired me. Richard Frazier White, Anthony Brewer White, Cheryl Ann White, my daughter-in-law Dr. Aline Magnoni, my "adopted" daughter Renee Brewer, and my Godchildren Jackie Beach and Rebeka Beach have read several pages of this book and given me their thoughts. My poems have been used at the weddings of my children. This book is a legacy for my grandchildren whether by birth or adoption: Lucas Antonia Romanini White, Sofia Giulia Romanini White, Doryan Kristjan Beach, Jonah Kaj Beach, Mikah Pierce Beach, and Mariahna Nickole Kellum. They inspire me.

To each of you who cherish the expressions of one's beliefs, feelings, emotions, and prayers on paper.

Introduction

I love poetry. I love the rhythmic beat in poems. I like the rhyming words of poems. When reading, reciting, or listening to poetry, I love the pictures conjured up in my mind.

I have been writing poems, it seems, all my life. I started in elementary school with simple four-line rhyming poems. I liked to play with words to find the best rhymes or the best rhythms. I think my love for poetry came about because I imitated Mother.

Mother loved poetry so much! She liked reciting the poems either from memory or reading from her notebook of poems she had collected. I liked for Mother to read aloud. She was gifted in the oral art of storytelling. Mother was an excellent reader. She read with inflection and enthusiasm. Each night before bedtime, she read to us from such children's classics as *Heidi* by Johanna Spyri, *Black Beauty* by Anna Sewell, *Little Women* by Louisa May Alcott, and *Rebecca of Sunnybrook Farm* by Kate Douglas Wiggin. Filled with unforgettable characters, these books were enjoyable and Mother's reading brought those characters to life. We cried when the stories got sad and we laughed and cheered when there were triumphs. As Mother spoke, I could "see" vivid pictures of the characters in the poem or story. As Mother read to us, her inflections made the experience so real that our emotions ebbed and flowed with the tempo of her voice and the intensity of those vicarious events. Those emotions made us want to listen every night as Mother recited or read. It was so real! If the piece were sad, we cried. If it were happy, we laughed – out loud! Yes, vicariously, we lived rich full lives through those stories and poems. They created deeper appreciation for living!

Mother also read poems and Bible stories. She taught us to memorize poems and scripture passages. The first memory verses after graduating from "Jesus wept" (John 11:35, KJV) were from Psalm 23 (KJV). Night after night, we recited what Mother taught us until we knew the entire passages "by heart" and could recite them at will. By the time I was in the fourth grade, Mother taught us to memorize longer pieces such as "If" by Rudyard Kipling and "A Psalm of Life" by Henry Wadsworth Longfellow. In sixth grade, I memorized Ecclesiastes 3, Verses 1-8 (KJV). In eleventh grade, I memorized (from William Shakespeare's Hamlet) Polonius' letter of advice to his son, Laertes, who was about to leave home for France.

Over the years, I graduated to more reflective writings in verse or prose. I try to find the beauty in every moment – even "when things go wrong, as they sometimes will." When I find the beauty, I write about it. I have written about such dichotomies as love, loneliness, losses, and dreams. Through poetry, I have experienced life in many aspects.

Recently, I learned about **Haiku**, Japanese poetry. In simple form, it consists of three phrases. The first phrase consists of five morae (syllables); the second phrase consists of seven syllables; and the third phrase consists of five syllables. It is very challenging for me to say something meaningful in just 17 syllables. This 5-7-5 pattern is one type of Haiku. Several Haiku poems are scattered throughout this book. The challenge was fun!

I love poetry. Sunday evenings, Daddy and Mother would sit on the sofa in the living room and listen to us recite poems, scripture, or sing songs that we had been taught by Mother through the week. We called it "Program Night" and we enjoyed reciting to that very appreciative audience of two. Dad was especially demonstrative of appreciation for our "renditions" on Program Night. He taught us how to stand, hold our hands, and take a bow. Mother looked happy about her charges carrying on a tradition she loved. She told us of the oratorical contests in which she competed. She related one of her greatest sorrows was dropping to second place because she swallowed during her recitation. It was a healthy childhood filled with literature and music.

Contents

A Certain Reality

Thinking of You ....
    When I think of you
    As I so often do,
    I start to contemplate.

Deeper thought ....
    My mind goes afar,
    As through a door left ajar -
    Open to welcome debate.

The Debate ....
    Is this a dream?
    Are things what they seem?
    Where is reality?

Their Reality ....
    "Dreams can't be real.
    Trust only what you feel,"
    They say with finality.

Introspection ....
    But I know my heart.
    I know every part.
    And these things, for me, are true...

My Reality ....
    That "real" is no measure
    Of my heart's treasure.
    My reality is a dream of you.

Haiku – The Son Shine

The sun never sets
Upon the Kingdom of God.
The Son always shines.

The Kiss

I have experienced your kiss
and it is so divine,
so gentle and revealing of
your tenderness.

Your kiss is like an emperor's seal
to mark and proclaim
your love for me.

I have experienced your kiss
so many times
and in so many places.

Your kiss is like a greeting
that says, "Come with me...
I want to mark time with you."

I have experienced your kiss
and it is like a promise
of infinite possibilities,
of joyous love,
of playful times,
of serious concern.

I have experienced your kiss
but only in a dream.

Haiku on Love

I'm falling in love!
With passion ever so strong,
How can it be wrong?

Lately

August 1995

Lately, I've been thinking
a lot about you.

Lately, I've been wondering
just what to do.

Lately, I've been thinking
my soul's in jeopardy.

Lately, I've been seeking
divine harmony. . .

Divine Harmony

This poem "Lately" was written as a caution to consider that a one-sided love relationship can do harm. You can be in love with someone too much for your own good. Your being in love fills your heart to the point of overflowing into all aspects of your life. You think often about how good it's going to be when your relationship grows strong. You dream of the day when there will be more open sharing of feelings, more evidence of caring, more of a *mutual* commitment to the relationship. Meanwhile, you are under the spell of your beloved. Wait!!! Before you give yourself to the point of no return, before you lay your greatest treasures out to be taken, stop and think what is happening to your soul. Is it really Love? Seek Divine Guidance to achieve Divine Harmony.

Haiku – Together in Love

Together at play
We learn the power of love
To meld our bodies.
We are together
Love holds us so surely here
We cherish this time

The Fantasy Director

In my fantasy, all is real.
Largely based on how I feel.
I'm the director of my dream.
I make things be the way they seem.
I'll choose the path that leads to where
I can live my life without a care.
I'll use my fantasy, my vision,
To direct every big or small decision.

Haiku – All Night Long

I love being here
Lying under the stars
Lounging with my love.

We pause briefly
To watch the night take leave and
Daybreak greet the sun.

Haiku – Alone at Night

I love being here
Lying under the stars
Waiting for my Love

I pause briefly
To watch the night take leave and
Daybreak greet the sun.

About the Poem Titled "Love"

I learned in Mrs. Howland's tenth grade geometry class that the strongest construction known to man is the triangle. A triangle can be pushed, shoved, or subjected to outside force and it will not change. That's why bridges and tall buildings have braces that form a triangle. Triangles are everywhere! The triangle with its three sides and three angles is a very strong thing.

That's how I see the God-focused **marriage – a triangle. With God** as the focal point, husband and wife see each other through their reflections from God. Hence, when a couple loves God, and they each look to God for answers, they see not each other's faults. God's love covers their faults and they learn to accept each other without so much criticism.

A True Love Triangle

Love

When a man loves a woman
And the source, the inspiration
Is obedience to God's command,
That love is a real celebration

When a woman loves a man,
And she cherishes his being,
Submission is a desire of hers.
Love alters her seeing.

When a couple loves God
And they look up to Him,
They see not each other's faults.
His love covers them.

For, love is a commandment.
To obey is a personal decision.
Freely given that we may give,
Love is God's ultimate provision.

Prayers for Families *(1983)*

Leader: *There are prayers that ought to be said. We are a blessed family. God's hand is upon us. There are prayers that ought to be said.*
Response: For whom should we pray?

Leader: *Pray for the elders. And not only our elders, pray for the elderly in all families.*
Response: In the gray years of life, Dear God, the elders need our prayers. Many are weary. Some are sick and in constant pain. There are those whose faith may not be as strong as it once was. We now hold them up in prayer. We pray for the elders.

Leader: *Pray for the parents. And not only the parents gathered here, pray for parents everywhere.*
Response: Give them strength. And not only that, give them love and courage to declare, as Joshua did, that they and their household will serve the Lord. Help the parents choose to love the Lord our God, to obey His word, and cling to Him so that they and their descendants may live. We pray for parents.

Leader: *Pray for the children. And not only these children, pray for all children.*
Response: Help them understand the promises of God. Let the children know that to obey their parents pleases the Lord. God has promised long life upon the earth to those who honor their father and their mother. Feed the children, Dear God, on your Word. For your Word is life and health to them. We pray for the children.

Leader: *Pray for love.*
Response: Our Heavenly Father, we love You because You first loved us. Help us to love others with the Love of God. For, if we love someone, we will be loyal to him or her. We will believe in them, always expecting the best of them, always standing ground in defending them. We pray for love.

Leader: *These prayers, Dear God, we submit to You. We thank You and praise You. In the name of Jesus, we pray.*

All: *Amen*

Haiku – The Godly Marriage

Love's so very sweet
We gladly invite God to
Wrap us in His Love.

A Haiku Poem

The ocean comes rolling
    Onto the shore with a crash,
        Then leaves all too soon.

Remembering Mother and Daddy in Poems

Mother and Daddy were very good parents – not perfect, but really good parents. I have started writing my memories of them in tribute and I titled it *Ordinary People, Extraordinary Parents*. Each of them taught us so much! Daddy was a motivator who inspired all seven of his children to get an education. Mother was a disciplinarian. A housewife, Mother was a teacher to her brood and she was very consistent. Both of them were gentle.

When we were children, Mother taught us to be creative in our play. Our dolls had names. We had tea parties. Mother taught us to hold the tea cup with three fingers, the thumb and two first fingers. Mother said that we should not stick out the left-over fingers. She knew someone who did that and Mother said sticking out fingers was "putting on airs" and was not proper. She taught us so much! When we were children, in case of bullies or childish taunts, Mother would say, "Don't pay them any attention. Just come on home." She was always waiting for us on the front porch. Mother was an invalid for over 20 years before she died in 1987 at the age of 67 years.

Daddy and Mother were a team. We could not play one against the other. Daddy would say, "What did your mother say?" Daddy was a teacher, too. He taught us his family history in stories from his childhood in the small town of Crofton, Kentucky. We knew our cousins. We learned so much from Daddy. He taught us to see the best in people, but if betrayed, to "Treat them nice, but keep on going."

Mother

She's walking now.
She's feeling better, somehow.
As God did say it would be,
Mother's new body is heavenly!

Some things she did not take
When that eternal journey she did make,
She left behind that old wheelchair
And set her eyes on Heaven's stair.

She did leave with us to keep
Memories of her love so deep.
She took so little and gave so much.
She'd say, "I love you" with a touch.

She made our house a HOME so fair.
Neighbor children gathered there.
All were welcomed and nurtured dear.
She made them happy just to be near.

She taught her children to kneel and pray
To tell God whatever they wanted to say.
She read to them from the Word of God
Truths that guide like a gentle rod.

We will see her again some day
When we go by that heavenward way.
Until then, from Heaven's front door dome,
Mother is saying, "Just come on home."

Daddy

He was a gentle man. He was kind. He was strong
He taught his children to know right from wrong.

Most of all, though, God guided his life.
He prayed and believed to overcome strife.

Daddy always said, "Listen to your Mother."
"Don't fight your sister." "Don't fight your brother."

Daddy taught us to withstand any test.
"You can do anything. Just give it your best."

When feeling betrayed and our hurt was showing,
Daddy said, "Just treat 'em nice, and keep on going."

Daddy gave each of us a sincere appreciation
For learning and the importance of an education.

He taught us to think and remember good, saying,
"Baby Dear, an understanding is a wonderful thing."

Beloved by his family and friends young and old,
Daddy was that treasure like silver and gold.

So when we celebrate all the "good old days,"
We remember Daddy and his gentle ways.

The Sunday School Teacher

She arises early
To teach of God's love,
To tell of redemption,
And prepare souls for above.

Little ones, big ones,
She teaches them all.
Fidgety ones, serene ones,
She answers the call.

She looks into each
Wonderful little face.
And teaches her charges
To sing of God's grace.

"Yes Jesus Loves Me,"
Children sing with conviction
As they learn of Jesus' life
And his crucifixion.

She teaches them to go
And tell many others
Starting with parents,
Then sisters and brothers.

She teaches how to live
And to freely share,
To never quarrel
And never despair.

For God is right with us.
We have only to pray
For guidance and
He will show us the way.

She teaches obedience,
To resist temptation,
She teaches the Bible -
Genesis to Revelation.

She teaches how to recite
Some memory verses,
To love their neighbors,
To overcome curses.

The experience of love
From this wonderful creature,
Is truly a gift from God -
She's your Sunday school teacher!

We were brought up in Sunday school at Brown Memorial C.M.E. Church and the Hughlette Temple A.M.E. Church in Louisville, Kentucky. Some of life's most important lessons in faith and prayer were learned in Sunday school. Many of those lessons are embodied in this poem. I have recited this poem for women and men. Just change "she" to "he" and "her" to "him" if you like. No matter the gender, all the characteristics of a Sunday school teacher still apply.

What Family Means to Me

(2004)

The family is a unit that grows through birth or adoption. United by a strong bond called "love," the family stands strong against many things that would break it apart. Some are stronger than others, but all are amazing. The value of family is...

Priceless...

The value of our family is priceless. It means we can come together at any time and be glad we each "belong" to this group. It means our needs are met. Not just food, water, and air. In the early years of life, it meant also guidance was provided and sometimes *applied* to the backside. In a big family such as ours, it meant sharing. We shared everything. We shared our faith in God. We shared our books. We shared our clothes. We slept in shared bedrooms. We ate around the same table. We shared conversations. We shared fights. We shared encouragement. We shared the air we breathed. **Roots and Wings...** Do you remember when you were growing up you thought you wanted to get as far away from home as possible? Funny thing is we didn't know our parents were wishing the same thing. So from that inner desire to break away, we spawned families of our own. I love my children dearly. And in loving them, I always want them to learn of their roots. Healthy families are like that. There is an old saying that the best things we can give to our children are roots and wings. Roots to hold firm to the living organism called family, and wings to soar above anything that would keep them from experiencing life for themselves.

Dynamics of Family . . .

Family means enjoying good times, like gathering around to swap tales. Sitting under a shade tree on weather-beaten chairs. Eating the food right off the grill. Drinking what has been hospitably presented. Hating to leave. Tired and worn out, we look forward to the time when we can do it all over again. Who says we can't all talk at the same time? We can do that and answer each other, too. It's a sophisticated way of multi-tasking. We don't always agree. In fact, we don't agree on lots of things. We even hurt each other at times. More than once we have delivered a sharp answer with cutting words. These things happen and we confront each other sometimes not in a loving way. Sometimes we just want to have our way. In the end, however, the glue that holds us together holds tight. We are family.

Firsts . . .

Many firsts take place in the family. We take our first steps and we learn to travel. We eat our first solid food and we learn about provision. We get our first hug and we learn about love. We have our first fight and we learn to defend our points of view. We have our first friends and we learn the value of teamwork. We get our first discipline and we learn about boundaries. We say our first words and we learn the value of expressions and communication. That's the way it is in a family. That's what it is like.

Never too Old to Dream

You're never too old to have a dream and work to make that dream come true.
You're never too old to share the best of whatever's inside of you.

The future belongs to each of us who stakes a claim starting today.
It's looking forward to what's to come and actively moving in that way.

To relinquish your dream because of age – fearing not getting to the end –
Is like surrendering a precious jewel to a thief instead of bequeathing it to a friend.

Dreams are not just for the young. They're for the young at heart.
They're for those who see possibilities and then give it a start.

Some folk look backward and then yearn for that "good old day".
Dreamers look forward with full belief that there must be a better way.

Dreamers don't listen to the voices that say, "It's too late." with finality.
Instead, they listen to the inner voice that says, "Pursue your reality."

You're never too old to have a dream. Your dream is your legacy.
That dream will take on a life of its own and travel to its own destiny.

So don't be ashamed of the fact that you dream and work to make your dreams come true.
Some of the most important inventions came from dreamers who were older than you.

God puts dreams into the minds of those He trusts to carry them out.
Your dream may be God's purpose for you, so go forth without a doubt.

When you give up thinking that you're too old to dream and act on your new belief,
You'll find the pursuit of that dream of yours to be fulfilling and such a relief.

My Personal Tear Bottle

(Based on Psalm 56:8)

My Personal tear bottle
Contains tears that I shed
I wrung out my pain
Through eyes that turned red.

My personal tear bottle
Is a heavenly gift
I fill it to the brim
Whenever there's a rift.

Those tears are not wasted
God catches every one
And puts them in that bottle
'til hurtful times are gone.

I thank God for that bottle
And all other provisions
He gives us to help
With life's big decisions.

He pours out that bottle
When watering is needed
Upon dry barren places
That with hope and love are seeded.

Those tears are life giving
When poured out like rain
And the bottle is ready
To be filled up again.

A Love Letter

My Dearest,

Good morning, my husband! You greeted me with a smile and a request. You said, "A penny for your thoughts!" So I decided to write you a letter after breakfast. These are some of my thoughts.

I think of you all the time. I am so joyous that we are in each other's lives. What are my thoughts? My thoughts are both sensual and spiritual because I both love you (spiritual) and I am in love with you (sensual).

I *love* you, and I am grateful that you are a *man of God.* To God is the Glory for His gifts of love and companionship. I always wanted a man who would be my spiritual partner in life. True Love comes from God and is experienced through our relationship with God.

I am *in love* with you. Dear, when I think of you and that very first kiss in the restaurant, my body tingles. You excite me! I trust you and have never been so willing to share all of me with someone. You are so strong and amazing! I get a warm glow from the top of my head to the tips of my toes. I want to experience so much with you.

We will keep cultivating joy and keep enjoying the simple yet sensual pleasures that life has to offer. Thoughts of you make everyday life more fun and enjoyable. Let's enjoy lots of things together – walking, movies, plays, musicals, travel, friends, and many more (some just spontaneous).

There's more. I can hardly wait to see you at the end of each day.

Love and Passion,
Julia

A dying art, the love letter is still a wonderful gift. The receiver can read it again and again. It can be stored under the pillow, in a box, or in the heart – wherever is most convenient for easy retrieval.

Family is Like . . .

It's so hard to describe what family means because it means more than we can put into few words. We can say what it is *like*. It is like so many things. A family is like a ...

- **Spring board.** Jump on it, and it launches you into your future
- **Cocoon** – Stay until just the perfect time to come into your own
- **Sanctuary** – The healthy home provides safety, shelter.
- **Army** – We may not all agree, but we stand together in a fight.
- **Tree** –Roots go down deep. Beauty is in the branches and leaves.
- **Nursery** – It is a fertile place for producing flowering lives.
- **Infirmary** – nurture for the sick or hurting comes from family.
- **Feast** –We are fed physically, morally, mentally and spiritually.
- **Iron** –The wrinkles in our personalities are made smooth.
- **Boardroom** – Life's most important decisions are made here.
- **Ocean** – There is no end to the love of family.
- **Boxing Ring** – We fight. At times we even bleed. We still love.
- **Old Shoe** – Taken for granted, yet held onto for dear life.
- **Nest** – We stay until we learn to fly. Then we fly to new heights.
- **Rubber Band** – We stretch out and return again in joyous reunion.
- **Journal** – The family story is written, one day at a time.
- **Puzzle** – The pieces fit. The picture eventually emerges.
- **Team** – Real strength comes from joint effort.
- **Job** – Sometime requires a lot of work.
- **Cruise** -- Sometimes the waters are choppy, sometimes smooth. Family keeps sailing.
- **Tree** – Grounded with good roots, watered with love, the branches keep growing and spreading. Family grows.

Charity: The Greatest Gift

1 Corinthians 13
King James Version (KJV)

Though I speak with the tongues of men and of angels, and have not charity, I am become as sounding brass, or a tinkling cymbal.

2 And though I have the gift of prophecy, and understand all mysteries, and all knowledge; and though I have all faith, so that I could remove mountains, and have not charity, I am nothing.

3 And though I bestow all my goods to feed the poor, and though I give my body to be burned, and have not charity, it profiteth me nothing.

4 Charity suffereth long, and is kind; charity envieth not; charity vaunteth not itself, is not puffed up,

5 Doth not behave itself unseemly, seeketh not her own, is not easily provoked, thinketh no evil;

6 Rejoiceth not in iniquity, but rejoiceth in the truth;

7 Beareth all things, believeth all things, hopeth all things, endureth all things.

8 Charity never faileth: but whether there be prophecies, they shall fail; whether there be tongues, they shall cease; whether there be knowledge, it shall vanish away.

9 For we know in part, and we prophesy in part.

10 But when that which is perfect is come, then that which is in part shall be done away.

11 When I was a child, I spake as a child, I understood as a child, I thought as a child: but when I became a man, I put away childish things.

12 For now we see through a glass, darkly; but then face to face: now I know in part; but then shall I know even as also I am known.

13 And now abideth faith, hope, charity, these three; but the greatest of these is charity.

கூ∾

Author note: Charity = Love. The greatest of these is Love.

A New Love

My love for you was so pure and true
I wanted very much to love only you.
I wanted you to know just what it meant
To experience a love that was Heaven-sent.
But now I feel cheated, alas, so alone.
I'll cry and I'll wonder just what went wrong.
But when I recover and want something else,
I'll find that real love starts with loving one's self.

When Trust is Gone

When trust is gone, I feel so alone.
I miss you so very, very much.
I miss your kiss, your warm tender touch.
When trust is gone.
When trust is gone, you don't look so strong.
I'm not in love with you anymore
When trust is gone.

Love Spurned

When I say to you, "I love you,"
And you say to me, "That's good,"
I wonder if you received my love
The way I hoped you would.
For love, when it is given
Is a calculated risk
And love, when returned
Is a little slice of heaven.

Haiku 3

Loving is risking.
     Hoping for true happiness,
          Love's its own reward.

Loneliness

I thank God for everything - even the loneliness. Never before in life have I been so lonely. Before, I never knew what loneliness really is. I thought I knew, but I also thought it could be dissipated through closer relationships with the people I knew - my parents, my husband, my children, my brothers

"All Alone"
Photo by Cheryl A. White

and sisters, and my close friends. Now I know I was wrong!

Loneliness is an affair of the heart - a spiritual matter. Loneliness can only be healed by a closer relationship with God. Just to know that I can talk to God about anything makes me not lonely.

So . . .

> When I'm feeling lonely,
> Like I've lost my way,
> I ask the Lord to guide me
> As I go through the day.
> I thank God for His goodness,
> His mercy, love, and peace.
> His gifts soothe my spirit
> And bid my sorrows cease.

Missing You

When you are gone,
And I'm all alone,
I miss talking with you.

My heart keeps yearning.
My passion is burning.
I miss being with you.

I think of our meeting,
And your special greeting.
I miss seeing you.

I think of you so much,
Your strong yet gentle touch.
I miss touching you.

When you're far away,
Not included in my day,
I miss sharing with you.

When we're out of touch,
Not speaking very much
I miss hearing from you.

When there is no phone call
No letter, nothing at all,
I miss learning from you.

When there is no visit,
I ask, 'Just what is it?"
I miss the presence of you.

Thinking across the miles
Brings me wistful smiles.
I'm still loving you.

Solitude

You may be standing
all alone
And feel that
you're really one.
But God is with you
all the while.
You are never alone.

So turn your
aloneness into time
That's filled
with gratitude.
You're not alone
when thankful to God.
You're just in solitude.

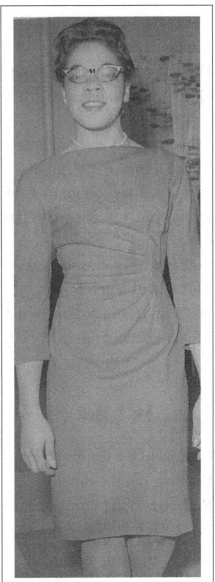

Standing All Alone
Julia Frazier White
Age 19

The Poet

I wrote it, so I get to read it,
I'm the one who knows
How to extract the meaning
Of my created prose.

I'll convey my every thought.
I want to make it clear
Just how I feel on many things
I want you, my friend, to hear.

So listen very closely now.
Then I will listen to you.
We'll understand, then, what we say.
Misunderstandings will be few.

Love Is Like . . .

Love is like a flaming fire
Burning out the dross,
Refining to the purest form.
What's left is gain – not loss.

Many Moods

There are times when I feel like singing.
There are times when my heart is winging.

There are times when I feel like crying.
There are times when I feel like dying.

There are times when I feel like sharing.
There are times when I feel like daring.

There are times when I feel like playing.
There are times when I feel like praying.

There are times when I feel like teaching.
There are times when I feel like preaching.

There are times when I feel like writing.
There are times when I feel like fighting.

There are times when I feel like talking.
There are times when I feel like walking.

There are times when I feel like drinking.
There are times when I feel like thinking.

There are times when I feel like knitting.
There are times when I feel like sitting.

There are times when I feel like sleeping.
There are times when I feel like weeping.

There are times . . .

Haiku 4

A gentle breeze blows
    Carrying your sweet perfume
        Right straight to my heart.

Pondering

In my aloneness, I ponder many thoughts of you.
I wonder why I feel left out and why I feel so blue.

I wonder why my every thought seems tuned to how you feel.
I wonderful if you know at all my loneliness is real?

So, then I had a meaningful, very long talk with me.
I said to self, "You're anything you ever want to be."

"So, hold your chin up, keep it up at a regal tilt.
And never let yourself get down. Don't let your spirit wilt."

Your esteem is not from what others think or define you to be.
Your personal worth is defined by you. Set your spirit free.

Free Spirit

I let my spirit go to soar as it sees fit.
I allowed my spirit to be totally free for a bit.
Oh, it's guarded and protected from really getting lost,
By angels, yes guardians, who know what spirits cost.
My spirit came back to me to resume residence.
It gives me great joy to rely on unseen evidence.

Ecclesiastes

To everything there is a season,

And a time to every purpose under the heaven:

A time to be born, and a time to die;

A time to plant, and a time to pluck up that which is planted;

A time to kill, and a time to heal;

A time to break down, and a time to build up;

A time to weep, and a time to laugh;

A time to mourn, and a time to dance;

A time to cast away stones, and a time to gather stones together;

A time to embrace, and a time to refrain from embracing;

A time to get, and a time to lose;

A time to keep, and a time to cast away;

A time to rend, and a time to sew;

A time to keep silence, and a time to speak;

A time to love, and a time to hate;

A time of war, and a time of peace.

Ecclesiastes 3, Verses 1-8 (KJV)
I memorized this passage for my sixth grade graduation. Our teacher, Mrs. Billie J. Daniels, had us each memorize it and we recited it as a choral reading. She explained that a choral reading was to be recited aloud in unison by the entire class. She taught us the meaning of the passage, how to stand erect, and how to recite the passage fluently. We practiced this so that by Graduation Day we were ready to do the choral reading with confidence!

On the Brink

About to jump into the mainstream of life, I stand on the brink. Far below is an unwelcoming sea of faces yelling, "Don't come in here. There is no room for you!" The noise of life rushing by was deafening and disconcerting. I can't stay here on the brink. To turn back would be like unraveling the fabric of my life or dismantling the progress I had made. Going back, I would pass the milestones that once gave me joy and the courage to reach for more milestones. I'm on the brink!

About to jump, I hesitate long enough to gain the courage to jump! I can't stay here on the brink. I'll take my place in the mainstream of life and learn to swim upstream. Yes, life seems fluid and flowing on! There are dangers, too – undercurrents of competition, fast flowing unforgiving falls, and muddy banks that inhibit progress. There are people swimming against the current in their struggles against alcoholism, abuse, and lack of understanding. Stay out of their way lest they push others into cesspools and unwanted entanglements. The brink is not a good camp ground.

Jump!

Now swim!

Upstream!

Note:

The first version of "On the Brink" was written my senior year of college. I was about to graduate and it was scary to think of not being in school. For sixteen years, school had been my vocation. Now I was about to go from that vocation to a life of unknown expectation with cautious excitement.

The Greatest Love

Cheryl A White
Sunday, September 2, 2012 at 2:57am

The vision is ever before my eyes
But it is yet for the appointed time
So I'll be patient and expectantly wait
For it in faith
That which He has promised
Is foreign to my eyes and ears
And beyond my ability to imagine

He Who has promised
Is faithful and just
To bring it to pass
As He has a plan for
Me to prosper and not harm me,
To give me hope and a future

He is the Good Shepherd going before me
In love, asking me to trust and believe
In Him

He knows my fears.
Understands my questions.
Forgives my obstinacy.
Has mercy on my stumbles.
And gives grace to my pride.

This is the greatest love I've ever known.
And He has promised me the gift of experiencing it
Through marriage
While I am yet enclosed and clothed in flesh.

I accept.

Conversation With God

"Oh, Lord, my loving God, I need You. I lost my job. I have children. I have responsibilities. I no longer have a husband. I feel so alone in this world."

"You are not alone, my child, do not grieve the Holy Spirit of God with such talk. You were sealed for the day of redemption. I will never leave you or forsake you."

"Thank you, God! I am alone, but no longer lonely. Your Love embraces me. I rest in your peace, but considering my circumstances, I sure do not understand this peace. Have I lost my mind, God?"

Then, God says, "It's a peace that surpasses understanding. It is a peace that will guard your heart and your mind in Christ Jesus. No, you have not lost your mind. Your mind is being guarded by My peace through Christ Jesus."

"That's a great thing, God, but I wonder how will I live and take care of my children? I have three children by birth and have taken in four others who needed a home full of love and discipline. "How will I take care of all these teenagers?

Still patiently answering my musings, God said, "I have never seen the righteous forsaken nor their seed go begging bread."

"Sounds good, Lord, but am I righteous? I don't feel righteous. What does it mean to be righteous? How is it measured? Some of my thoughts are not good wishes."

"You have your righteousness through Christ Jesus."

"Thank you, Lord. I am thankful that I have righteousness through Christ Jesus. So, how will I make ends meet? My children and I have many needs.

"I, the Lord your God, will supply all your needs according to My riches in glory by Christ Jesus. I, the Lord your God am able to bless you abundantly, so that in all things and at all times, having all that you need, you will be able to continue the good work with these young people. When you were a child, your parents supplied your needs according to their resources. All your needs were met. The children of millionaires had their needs supplied according to their parents' wealth. Now, I am your heavenly Father. I created the world and own everything in the world. I will supply all your needs according to My riches in glory by Christ Jesus."

"Blessed assurance, Jesus is mine. Thank you, God for this conversation. Thank you. Good night."

Haiku 9

Be the best you can
Keep on trying, keep striving
Your best gets better.

The Mind

The Mind is real. When it is used creatively and wisely . . .

It's the incubator for thoughts.
It's the repository of ideas,
It's the fertile ground for creativity.

It's the laboratory for applying wisdom.
It's the place where knowledge is kept.
It's where knowledge is spun into wisdom.

It's the controller of personality.
It's the maker of decisions.
It's the keeper of the conscience.

It's the director of pen strokes.
It's the writer of manuscripts.
It's the measurer of intelligence.

It's the guard against conflict.
It's the solver of problems.
It's the mender of relationships.

It's the container of roadmaps.
It's the detour around past hurts.
It's the memory album for vacations past.

It's the conceiver of beauty.
It's the creator of dreams.
It's the incubator of love.

My Prayer

Dear God, my heavenly Father. I praise and adore You. I worship You. I praise You, God, for being my God all by yourself. You do not need my help. I submit my will to your Will. You are awesome! Awesome! You have done and continue to do wonderful things in my life. When things do not look good, You make them good. I praise and adore You.

I confess, Dear God that I have not always done your will. I am sorry for what I have thought, said, or done that was not pleasing to You. I have developed some destructive habits which You warned against such as overextension in activities and sleep deprivation. You commanded us to take care of our bodies and to rest. Please forgive me, Lord. I thank You, Dear God, for your mercy and your caring. Thank You for your many benefits. Thank You for your Love, your guidance, and your protection from all harm. Thank You for all your goodness.

I ask You to keep my children, their spouses, my grandchildren, and unborn generations in your care. I thank You that they each come under the lordship of Jesus Christ. I pray for their needs and for the needs of friends, extended family, and government leaders. Lord God Almighty, we all need your guidance, your wisdom, your mercy, and your Love. I thank You for these and all blessings.

Dear God, You have given us so many promises in your Word. I confess those promises OUT LOUD throughout my house. Through faith I have hope and a future! Glory!!! God, You manifest yourself in circumstances that seem impossible to us. You have provided for us what we need. Should we find ourselves despairing over things bigger than we are, cause us to remember that the record of your accomplishments have not come to an end. Amen.

Your Servant,
Julia

An Account of Healing

An Excerpt from "How I Overcame an Incurable Disease!"

Being diagnosed with sickness or disease can be a traumatizing experience, especially when the doctors say there is no cure. Requiring courage, this is a journey from a sure appointment with death… to a divine meeting with Christ the Healer! My hope is that this account of healing will lift your faith to new heights!

Isaiah 53 states that redemption includes forgiveness of sin and *healing* of our bodies. As I read the Word and *believed* the promises of God, my faith grew stronger. Since I began this journey of walking by faith concerning my health, my faith has increased greatly! I have watched God do what He said He would do for those who believe. He said that with just a small bit of faith, we could speak to the mountain and have it removed. Jesus said in Mark 11:23, "*that whosoever shall say unto this mountain, Be thou removed... ...and does not doubt in his heart but believes that what he says will happen, it will be done for him.*" Hereby, Jesus instructs us to pray to God and *speak* to the mountain. Jesus did not tell us to ask Him to speak to our mountains. He commanded us to speak to our own mountains!

I have spoken to the mountain of disease and commanded it to be removed from my body. I have spoken bold words of healing to my flesh in the face of symptoms and contrary evidence. All glory to God! I also moved from fear to faith in the area of my finances. My career as a Manager of Development of computer systems at a Fortune 100 company ended abruptly due to a disease called Dermatomyositis. This rare disease strikes only 1 in 300,000 people. Characterized by excruciating pain, all the muscles, joints, connective tissue, and the skin were inflamed. I was forced to retire and live off a very small pension. It can be very disconcerting to go from a very high-paying job with stock options down to about one twelfth of that! I was forced to make drastic changes in my habits and diet. Trusting God more than ever, I stood on Philippians 4:19 that says, "*But my God **shall supply all your needs according to his riches in glory by Christ Jesus.***" I continued to tithe and give to others in need. God has kept me in perfect peace. All my needs are supplied! I am on no medication! Doctors have declared me free of this "incurable" disease. Praise God!

Some Parental Wisdom

Can't find your gloves? Just keep looking. They'll be in the last place you look.   -- Alyce Virginia Brewer Frazier

Baby Dear, when people don't do right by you, still treat them nice, but keep on going. Don't waste your time with them. Just keep on going.   -- Latham Norvell Frazier

Want to retaliate? Kill 'em with kindness. It allows you to still be yourself and it confuses and shames your enemies.
         − Alyce Virginia Brewer Frazier

Always wear a smile. It makes your entire outfit look better.
         − Alyce Virginia Brewer Frazier

Children, don't judge others because everyone has a story.
         − Rebeka Pia Syberg Beech

Take your time.
         − Anthony Brewer White

You can choose to stay positive.
         − Aline Magnoni

Do you know why you are called "grandchildren" instead of just children? It's because you are so grand.
         − Lizzy Beatrice Frazier (Grandmother)

The 23rd Psalm

The LORD is my shepherd; I shall not want.

He maketh me to lie down in green pastures: he leadeth me beside the still waters.

He restoreth my soul: he leadeth me in the paths of righteousness for his name's sake.

Yea, though I walk through the valley of the shadow of death, I will fear no evil: for thou art with me; thy rod and thy staff they comfort me.

Thou preparest a table before me in the presence of mine enemies: thou anointest my head with oil; my cup runneth over.

Surely goodness and mercy shall follow me all the days of my life: and I will dwell in the house of the LORD forever.

Note;

Also known to us as "The Lord Is My Shepherd" in childhood, this is one of the first pieces that Mother taught us to memorize. It was a comforting psalm to us as children because Daddy and Mother told us to remember the part that said, "… thou art with me; thy rod and thy staff they comfort me." Also, the promise of goodness and mercy following us all the days of our lives painted the same mental picture as Mother and Daddy following us when we went for walks on Sunday afternoons. We did not have a car until years later. We walked to church. We walked to school. We walked to the local hardware store. Daddy walked to work at Butterman's Ice Cream Plant (later Borden's Ice Cream Company). We walked to the A&P Store. We walked everywhere and we were not afraid because we knew that Goodness and Mercy would be right with us at all times.

Brotherly Love

Beloved, let us love one another:

for love is of God;

and every one that loveth is born of God,

and knoweth God.

He that loveth not knoweth not God;

for God is love.   - 1 John 4:7-8

Haiku 8

Brotherhood is good
It's meant for all mankind
All can share the love.

Haiku – At the Ocean

The Atlantic ebbs
Away and comes back again,
Welcome the high tide.

Psalm 139

¹ O LORD, You have searched me and known *me.*
² You know my sitting down and my rising up;
    You understand my thought afar off.
³ You comprehend my path and my lying down,
    And are acquainted with all my ways.
⁴ For *there is* not a word on my tongue,
    But behold, O LORD, You know it altogether.
⁵ You have hedged me behind and before,
    And laid Your hand upon me.
⁶ *Such* knowledge *is* too wonderful for me;
    It is high, I cannot *attain* it.

⁷ Where can I go from Your Spirit?
    Or where can I flee from Your presence?
⁸ If I ascend into heaven, You *are* there;
    If I make my bed in hell, behold, You *are there.*
⁹ *If* I take the wings of the morning,
    And dwell in the uttermost parts of the sea,
¹⁰ Even there Your hand shall lead me,
    And Your right hand shall hold me.
¹¹ If I say, "Surely the darkness shall fall on me,"
    Even the night shall be light about me;
¹² Indeed, the darkness shall not hide from You,
    But the night shines as the day;
    The darkness and the light *are* both alike *to You.*

¹³ For You formed my inward parts;
    You covered me in my mother's womb.
¹⁴ I will praise You, for I am fearfully *and* wonderfully made.
    Marvelous are Your works,
    And *that* my soul knows very well.

Note:
Psalm 139 (vs. 1-14, KJV) is one of my favorite psalms. I take comfort in the fact that this Psalm 139 tells me that God is omnipotent, omnipresent, and omniscient. He's everywhere - omnipresent (vs. 7 – 12). He is all powerful – omnipotent (vs. 13-14). He has unlimited knowledge such that His knowledge is "… too wonderful for me and so high that I cannot *attain* it" (vs.6). What a mighty God!

Trees

I was in fifth grade when I fell in love with a simple poem titled *Trees*. I first read it on back of one of those funeral home paper fans found in a church pew. I committed it to memory. Each Sunday, I looked for just the right fan so that I could test my memory and discover any more "facts" about trees. I think what I really liked, because it was new to me, was the personification of the tree.

I Forgive You

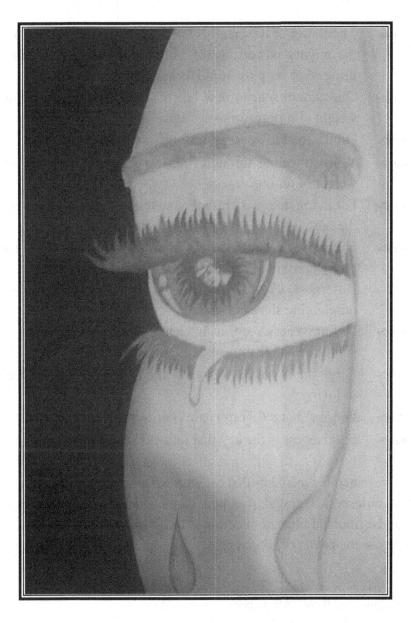

"I Forgive You"
Pencil and Charcoal Drawing
by
Cheryl A. White

Forgiveness Quotations by Julia

❧ ❧ The Power of Reversal! He has taught us forgiveness, and the mighty power thereof. He gave us this gift to undo things that keep us from His love.

❧ ❧ One cannot soar to new heights when held down by the weight of unforgiveness.

❧ ❧ On the road to Success, unforgiveness is a roadblock

❧ ❧ When traveling through life, travel light. Leave out the weight of unforgiveness.

❧ ❧ Forgiving does not erase the memory of the hurt. It erases the hurt.

❧ ❧ Unforgiveness is slavery in its worse form. There are too many masters to serve. Some are Hatred, Worthlessness, Bitterness, Fear, Depression, and Ugliness. These are unrelenting slave masters.

❧ ❧ Unforgiveness keeps us hitched up to the past as surely as if bridled and tied to a hitching post.

❧ ❧ Forgiving is not easy, but it is the easiest way to get back to loving.

❧ ❧ Forgive! Forget! Forgo pain! Forever!

❧ ❧ Forgiveness is the key that unlocks the heart to Love.

As we remember incidents that caused such powerful feelings as pain, fear, bitterness, betrayal, rejection, disgust, depression, jealousy, we may be troubled beyond our limits. To be free of such burdens, we may use the power of forgiveness.

Quotations and thoughts from book:

White, J. F. (2010). *Forgiveness: Learning How to Forgive.* Bloomington, IN: Xlibris Corporation.

Trust

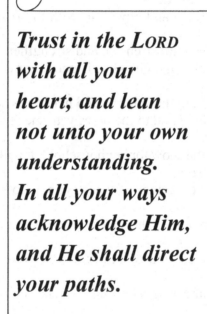

*Trust in the LORD
with all your
heart; and lean
not unto your own
understanding.
In all your ways
acknowledge Him,
and He shall direct
your paths.*

❧

Proverbs 3: 5-6

The Virtuous Woman

(Proverbs 31: 10-31 KJV)

Who can find a virtuous woman? for her price is far above rubies.

[11] The heart of her husband doth safely trust in her, so that he shall have no need of spoil.

[12] She will do him good and not evil all the days of her life.

[13] She seeketh wool, and flax, and worketh willingly with her hands.

[14] She is like the merchants' ships; she bringeth her food from afar.

[15] She riseth also while it is yet night, and giveth meat to her household, and a portion to her maidens.

[16] She considereth a field, and buyeth it: with the fruit of her hands she planteth a vineyard.

[17] She girdeth her loins with strength, and strengtheneth her arms.

[18] She perceiveth that her merchandise is good: her candle goeth not out by night.

[19] She layeth her hands to the spindle, and her hands hold the distaff.

[20] She stretcheth out her hand to the poor; yea, she reacheth forth her hands to the needy.

[21] She is not afraid of the snow for her household: for all her household are clothed with scarlet.

[22] She maketh herself coverings of tapestry; her clothing is silk and purple.

[23] Her husband is known in the gates, when he sitteth among the elders of the land.

[24] She maketh fine linen, and selleth it; and delivereth girdles unto the merchant.

[25] Strength and honour are her clothing; and she shall rejoice in time to come.

[26] She openeth her mouth with wisdom; and in her tongue is the law of kindness.

[27] She looketh well to the ways of her household, and eateth not the bread of idleness.

[28] Her children arise up, and call her blessed; her husband also, and he praiseth her.

[29] Many daughters have done virtuously, but thou excellest them all.

[30] Favour is deceitful, and beauty is vain: but a woman that feareth the LORD, she shall be praised.

[31] Give her of the fruit of her hands; and let her own works praise her in the gates.

My Smile

My smile doesn't mean I like you.
In fact, I may not even know you.

My smile means that I like me!
It's a reflection of what I think of me.

My smile says there is joy inside.
There is peace and plenty love inside.

My smile, like an ember brightly aglow
May just spark your heart and set it aglow.

The Whisper

One day, I had a very long talk with me.
I wondered, "Just what is it you want to be?"
I'll answer that question as soon as I know.
Meanwhile, it's important that I grow.
I must grow in the likeness of Christ
And never by the devil be enticed.
Then a small voice in the middle of my being
Whispers to me, "Peace. Be still."
It tells me, "Even in the midst of great turmoil,
Just be still and watch for God's will."

Haiku 6

Your touch is so sweet.
Unbelievable, but true,
I want only you.

Children of Promise - A Parent's Prayer

Children of Promise

*Each child has a promise from God.
It is up to us as parents to ignite the spark that enables
that child to burn with desire to achieve his or her full
potential – to come into full realization of that promise.
It is my prayer to have the patience, foresight, love, and
Godly wisdom to guide each child with joy. Amen.*

A Better Place

(Upon the death of my sister, Joyce Lavonne Frazier Stout)

She's in a better place They say,
A place They have not seen.
They use those words to comfort us,
Not trying to demean.
She's in a better place, They say.
A place of peace and love.
They say she made a journey
To live forever above.
She's in a better place They say.
A place of perfect tranquility.
They say she transitioned peacefully
To live forever in eternity.
She's in a better place, They say.
Where singing never ends.
Not wanting to return here,
She waits there for family and friends.
She's in a better place, They say.
A place where God himself is host.
They say Ultimate Love welcomed her
She loved each of us, but loved God most.

Haiku for Joyce

To feel her soft touch
And experience her love
Is a joy divine.

Though she has no breath,
Her love envelops us and....
Did not end with death.

The Ten Commandments

1. *Thou shalt have no other gods before me.*
2. *Thou shalt not make unto thee any graven image, or any likeness of anything.*
3. *Thou shalt not take the name of the Lord thy God in vain.*
4. *Remember the Sabbath day, to keep it holy.*
5. *Honour thy father and thy mother.*
6. *Thou shalt not kill.*
7. *Thou shalt not commit adultery.*
8. *Thou shalt not steal.*
9. *Thou shalt not bear false witness against thy neighbor.*
10. *Thou shalt not covet anything that is thy neighbor's.*

Note: As children, we were taught The Ten Commandments. It was the rule of law in our home.

My Prayer to Show Forth . . .

Heavenly Father, you, through Jesus Christ, have not only shown me love. You ARE Love. You have loved me so I can show forth your love. Thank you for your never ending, unconditional love. Lord, help me to be merciful, gracious, forgiving and loving.

With this love, I will, through grace, show mercy. For You extend new mercy to me every day (Lamentations 3:23), and as You are touched with the feeling of our infirmities (Hebrews 4:15), I will also rejoice with those who rejoice and weep with those who weep (Romans12:15).

With this love, I will forgive others as often as is necessary for who am I to deny forgiveness when Christ has forgiven me. "And be ye kind one to another, tenderhearted, forgiving one another, even as God for Christ's sake hath forgiven you" (Ephesians 4:32).

With this love, I will by your grace, love everyone even my enemies and those who despitefully use me (Matthew 5:44). I will, in fact, love others as Christ has loved me. This is not without sacrifice as God's love for me caused Him to die for me through Jesus Christ. "A new commandment I give unto you, that ye love one another; as I have loved you, that ye also love one another" (John 13:34).

Thank you, Christ, for your goodness, love, forgiveness and kindness. May I be more like you each day as I step back and allow you to step forward in my life and direct my steps toward your plan for my life. Amen.

Your Servant,
Julia

Haiku 7

I will not gossip
    I'll not backbite or defame.
        We love your good name.

It's All About Love

From Genesis to Revelation.
We learn of God's Love
And the joy of salvation.
It's all about Love.

We learn the power of love
As we share it with others,
To make for ourselves
Beloved sisters and brothers

When the strangest of friends
With love become united.
Demographics don't matter
They become single-sighted.

They are blessed to relate.
The relationship is sealed
With love that is a powerful,
Wondrous God-given shield

Depression Conquered

Drowning in sorrow and pity for myself,
I felt justified to spiral down to depression.
After all, I had never retaliated,
Nor resorted to any form of aggression.

Although I think I'm a nice person,
Anguish is my facial expression.
Why can't I escape this gloom?
Why is pain my constant confession?

I tried to think happy thoughts,
But I'm reminded of transgressions.
I thought I had remembered them no more.
Instead, I'm living with this oppression.

In prayer, I learned to change my thinking.
Was this gloom real or some obsession?
The gloom loomed large, enveloping me,
Pulling me further into regression.

Down, I spiraled to a point so very low,
I surrendered to deep depression.
My chest felt heavy, I could not breathe.
I needed relief from this compression.

I needed help to rise above the prison
Of this consuming and utter suppression.
I spoke sincere prayers that lifted my soul.
Now prayer is my constant confession.

Printed in the United States
By Bookmasters